Audit Report

Report Number: OIG-SBLF-13-002

STATE SMALL BUSINESS CREDIT INITIATIVE: Michigan's Use of Federal Funds for Capital Access and Other Credit Support Programs

December 13, 2012

Office of Inspector General

Department of the Treasury

Contents

Results In Brief 2
Background 4
    The State of Michigan's Participation in SSBCI 5
Michigan Generally Used SSBCI Funds Properly, but Misused $2.524 Million 7
    Michigan Business Growth Fund Financed $2.5 Million in Lender Purchases that Did Not Extend Credit to Borrowers 8
    Michigan Spent $3,000 on a Loan Used for a Prohibited Business Purpose 10
    Michigan Paid $21,000 for a CAP Loan Prior to the State's Admission to the SSBCI Program .. 11
A Portion of Administrative Costs Were Not Allowable or Allocable 12
Recommendations 13
Appendix 1: Objective, Scope, and Methodology 17
Appendix 2: Management Response 19
Appendix 3: Major Contributors 31
Appendix 4: Distribution List 32

Abbreviations

    CAP   Capital Access Program
    OIG   Office of Inspector General
    OMB   Office of Management and Budget
    MEDC   Michigan Economic Development Corporation
    MSF   Michigan Strategic Fund
    SSBCI   State Small Business Credit Initiative
    The Act   Small Business Jobs Act of 2010

OIG

The Department of the Treasury
Office of Inspector General

Audit Report

December 13, 2012

Don Graves, Jr.
Deputy Assistant Secretary for Small Business, Housing, and Community Development

This report presents the results of our audit of the State of Michigan's use of funds awarded under the State Small Business Credit Initiative (SSBCI), which was established by the Small Business Jobs Act of 2010 (the Act). In June 2011 Michigan was awarded approximately $79.1 million,[1] of which $4.2 million was allocated to the Michigan Capital Access (CAP) Program, $68.9 million was allocated to the Michigan Business Growth Fund, and $6 million went to the Small Business Mezzanine Fund. As of March 2012, the State had received the first two disbursements of funding totaling approximately $52.2 million, and had obligated or spent approximately $38.5 million on loans enrolled either in the CAP or the Michigan Business Growth Fund.

The Act requires the Treasury Office of Inspector General (OIG) to conduct audits of the use of funds made available under SSBCI and to identify any instances of reckless or intentional misuse. Treasury has defined reckless misuse as a use of funds that the participating state or administering entity should have known was unauthorized or prohibited, and which is a highly unreasonable departure or willful disregard from the standards of ordinary care. Intentional misuse is any unauthorized or prohibited use of funds that the participating state or its administering entity knew was unauthorized or prohibited.

Our audit objective was to test participant compliance with program requirements and prohibitions to identify any reckless or intentional

---

[1] Rounded down from the actual award amount of $79,157,742.

misuse of funds. We reviewed a statistical sample of 36 small business loans enrolled in the Michigan CAP and 23 small business loans enrolled in the Michigan Business Growth Fund prior to December 31, 2011. We reviewed the loans to determine whether they complied with program requirements for loan use, capital at risk, and other restrictions. We also reviewed the administrative costs charged against SSBCI funds related to these programs to ensure they were accurate and supported in accordance with Treasury Guidelines and Office of Management and Budget (OMB) Circular A-87, *Cost Principles for State, Local, and Indian Tribal Governments*. We visited the offices of the Michigan Economic Development Corporation (MEDC), the administrative entity that was given program responsibility for overseeing the use of SSBCI funds in Michigan. All loan files sampled from the applicable lending institutions were directly forwarded to us electronically or provided to us on site at MEDC. Appendix 1 contains a more detailed description of our audit objective, scope, and methodology.

We conducted our audit from April 2012 to November 2012 in accordance with *Government Auditing Standards.* Those standards require that we plan and perform the audit to obtain sufficient, appropriate evidence to provide a reasonable basis for our findings and conclusions based on our audit objective. We believe that the evidence obtained to address our audit objective provides a reasonable basis for our findings and conclusions.

Results In Brief

Our sample results suggest that the majority of the $38.5 million in SSBCI funds obligated or expended by the State of Michigan prior to December 31, 2011, was used properly. However, we identified approximately $2.524 million in misuse, of which:

- $2.5 million was used to finance lender purchase transactions that did not involve extensions of additional credit to borrowers;

- $3,000 supported a partner buy-out, a prohibited purpose; and

- $21,000 was used to pay the CAP insurance premium on a loan closed and funded prior to Michigan's acceptance into the SSBCI program and Treasury's allocation of funds to the State.

We determined that $21,000 of the $2.524 million constituted a "reckless" misuse of funds as defined by Treasury guidance, which under the provisions of the Small Business Jobs Act must be recouped. While we did not find that the $2.5 million in lender purchases constituted reckless misuse, we questioned whether loan purchase transactions that do not increase capital to new businesses are consistent with the intent of the Act to help small businesses expand, grow, and create jobs. Therefore, Treasury will need to develop guidance for such transactions. We also noted that Michigan's application was worded so broadly that it allowed the State to use its SSBCI funds to help a failing business, which was an exception from how it stated it anticipated using its SSBCI funds. We did not find the $3,000 supporting a partner buy-out to be a reckless or intentional misuse because even though the purpose of the loan was clearly prohibited, State officials were unaware of the loan's purpose, as the loan enrollment form they reviewed and signed did not disclose the loan's purpose.

Additionally, we found that $8,506 of administrative costs charged to the SSBCI program was incurred prior to June 21, 2011, the date Michigan was approved to participate in SSBCI and notified of its SSBCI allocation. As a result, the $8,506 was not allowable or properly allocable to the program.

We recommend that Treasury recoup from Michigan the $21,000 identified as a reckless misuse of funds, and disallow $8,506 in administrative expenses. We also recommend that Treasury issue guidance addressing the conditions under which loan purchase transactions would be permissible, and require Michigan to modify its application to require that any exceptions granted to its anticipated use of funds be documented and approved by Treasury to ensure they are made for good causes and in a manner that is consistent with the intent of the Act. Finally, we recommend that Treasury require states that grant funds as exceptions to their own stated policies to provide written justification for doing so, and that it require states to use enrollment forms for CAP programs that disclose the purpose of the loans enrolled.

Treasury accepted each of our recommendations. Although Treasury believes that Michigan's purchase of a loan participation was not prohibited and was consistent with its approved State program, Treasury will issue guidance addressing the conditions under which loan purchase transactions would be permitted. It will also require Michigan to acknowledge that it will document and seek approval for any use of funds that differs from its original SSBCI application, and require states to provide written justification when using SSBCI funds in a way that differs from their applications. Further, Treasury will recoup from Michigan $21,000 for enrolling a loan that a financial institution closed prior to Michigan's participation in the program, and require states to use enrollment forms for CAP programs that disclose the purpose of loans. Treasury will also disallow the $8,506 in impermissible administrative expenses.

Background

SSBCI is a $1.5 billion Treasury program that provides participating states, territories, and eligible municipalities with funding to strengthen CAPs and other credit support programs that provide financial assistance to small businesses and manufacturers. CAPs provide portfolio insurance for business loans based on a separate loan loss reserve fund for each participating financial institution. Other credit support programs include collateral support, loan participation, loan guarantee, and venture capital programs. Each participating state is required to designate specific departments, agencies, or political subdivisions to implement the programs approved for funding. The designated state entity distributes the SSBCI funds to various public and private institutions, which may include a subdivision of another state, a for-profit entity supervised by the state, or a non-profit entity supervised by the state. These entities use funds to make loans or provide credit access to small businesses.

Primary oversight of the use of SSBCI funds is the responsibility of each participant. To ensure that funds are properly controlled and expended, the Act requires that Treasury execute an Allocation Agreement with participants setting forth internal controls, and compliance and reporting requirements before allocating SSBCI funds. SSBCI disbursements to participating states are made in three tranches: the first when the Secretary approves the state for participation, and the second and third after the participating state certifies that it has obligated, transferred, or spent at least 80 percent of the previous tranche. In addition, the participating state is required to certify that it has complied with all applicable program requirements.

The State of Michigan's Participation in SSBCI

On June 21, 2011, Treasury approved Michigan's application for the Michigan CAP, Michigan Business Growth Fund, and Small Business Mezzanine Fund programs, and awarded the State a total of $79,157,742. On July 8, 2011, Treasury disbursed the first of the State's allocation, $26,122,055, and on January 11, 2012, Treasury approved disbursement of the State's second allocation, $26,122,055. As of March 31, 2012, Michigan had obligated or spent $38,566,045, representing all of the first tranche and $12,443,990 of the second tranche. The State also used $198,811 of the $38,566,045 to pay administrative costs associated with implementing the State programs.

The Governor of Michigan designated the Michigan Strategic Fund (MSF) to receive SSBCI funds and administer the program under the Allocation Agreement with the U.S. Treasury. The MSF operates as an autonomous entity within the Michigan Department of Treasury. A Memorandum of Understanding was executed between the MSF and the MEDC, pursuant to which MEDC staff provide certain SSBCI administrative services to the MSF, subject to the direction and control of the MSF. The MSF is authorized to use allocated SSBCI funds only for the purposes and activities specified in the State's Allocation Agreement with Treasury, including for direct and indirect administrative costs.

Michigan CAP. The MSF established the Michigan CAP in 1986, and it operated until 2002. In 2005, State law directed the MSF to re-establish CAP as part of the State's loan enhancement program. CAP, at its peak, participated in over 1,000 loans per year and cost the MSF approximately $2 million per year to operate. MSF's cost was principally for loan insurance premiums.

Each loan that a participating financial institution enrolls in the Michigan CAP is protected by a reserve account in the institution's name. The reserve is funded through a one-time premium paid into the reserve in equal parts by the borrower and the lender. The MSF then matches the combined premium. The lender selects a premium, from 1.5 percent to 3.5 percent of the loan amount, based on the lending institution's assessment of the risk of the loan.

Michigan's Allocation Agreement provided up to $4.2 million in SSBCI funds to support Michigan's CAP. As of March 31, 2012, $340,901 of SSBCI funds had been expended for CAP insurance premiums for 167 loans with a total value of $10,454,685.

Michigan Business Growth Fund. In 2009, prior to the receipt of SSBCI funds, the MSF created the Michigan Supplier Diversification Fund to provide State funding in support of private lending activities. The State designed the fund to provide credit opportunities for Michigan suppliers that may not qualify for credit through traditional lenders. The Michigan Supplier Diversification Fund assisted in the underwriting of 20 separate lending facilities until State funds were substantially expended in April 2011.

In May 2011, the MSF established the Michigan Business Growth Fund to administer SSBCI funds approved for use in other credit support programs. The Michigan Business Growth Fund is a combined collateral support program and loan participation program. Collateral support programs help viable businesses that are struggling to get credit because the value of the collateral they hold has fallen, possibly due to the decline of commercial real estate values. Loan participation programs entail risk sharing among financial institution lenders and the State. Other credit support programs must demonstrate a 1:1 private leveraging ratio, meaning that each dollar of investment by the State must result in at least one dollar of new private credit.

The Allocation Agreement provided up to $68,957,742 in SSBCI funds for MSF's collateral support and loan participation programs. As of March 31, 2012, $14,244,319 of this amount had been expended for collateral support on 21 small business loans with a total value of $48,888,935. Additionally, the MSF directly lent an additional $18,816,020 to small businesses via 18 loan participation transactions totaling $42,180,937.

The Small Business Mezzanine Fund Program. The MSF has run a mezzanine fund program in the State since 2006 and has committed $17.5 million in State funds to support $460 million raised in the private sector for such financings. Michigan's Allocation Agreement with Treasury provides up to $6 million in SSBCI funds in support of this program. The State has been in talks with three capital formation groups that are raising mezzanine funds focused on small industrial technology and growth service sector firms. However, as of March 31, 2012, the MSF had not spent or obligated any SSBCI funds on this program.

Michigan Generally Used SSBCI Funds Properly, but Misused $2.524 Million

Of the 59 loans sampled, 55, or approximately 93 percent, complied with SSBCI program requirements. However, we identified $2.524 million that was misused on two loans enrolled in Michigan's CAP and two loans enrolled in Michigan's Business Growth Fund. The two loans enrolled in the Business Growth Fund were used to finance $2.5 million in lender purchase transactions that did not involve extensions of additional credit to borrowers. Another loan provided $3,000 for a business purpose prohibited under the Small Business Jobs Act. The remaining loan of $21,000 was made prior to Michigan's acceptance into the SSBCI program. However, only $21,000 met the Department's definition of "reckless misuse." The Act requires Treasury to recoup funds that were recklessly misused.

Michigan Business Growth Fund Financed $2.5 Million in Lender Purchases that Did Not Extend Credit to Borrowers

Michigan provided $2.5 million of SSBCI funds to a lender through its Michigan Business Growth Fund that was used to jointly purchase with the State two loans from another lender. The purchase was made to prevent the borrower, which was in bankruptcy, from being liquidated until it was purchased by an out-of-state private equity firm. The loan purchases also benefitted the prior lender by removing bad loans from its books. The new lender benefitted too by recouping, with interest, the funds it had loaned when the borrower's business was sold months after the loan purchases. Finally, the State recouped the SSBCI funds used to purchase the loans.

The loan purchases constituted a misuse of funds because they did not provide new credit or a cash infusion to the borrower, but rather transferred an existing loan from one lender to another. Thus, the transaction was not unlike a lender selling a home mortgage to another financial institution with no involvement by the borrower. However, the purchases helped the company avert chapter 7 bankruptcy and attract a buyer (although the company remains in chapter 11 bankruptcy). Because SSBCI Policy Guidelines do not address this type of transaction, we relied on our interpretation of the intent of the Act, as states must comply with both the Act and SSBCI Policy Guidelines.

While the transactions temporarily kept the borrower from defaulting on its two loans, we question whether loan purchases are consistent with the intent of the Act to increase capital to allow small businesses to expand, grow, and create jobs. If such transactions are allowed, SSBCI funds could be used to largely finance repeated loan purchases that do not increase the amount of capital extended to small businesses. While Treasury considers an increase in credit on a lender's books to constitute "new credit," regardless of whether the small business is advanced new monies, viewing this issue solely from the lender perspective could lead to sanctioning transactions that result in no net increases in lending or capital to small businesses. It would also allow Treasury to measure the success of the program by the amount of existing debt transferred from one lender to another, instead of the amount of capital that is made available to small businesses. Therefore, Treasury will need to issue guidance addressing the conditions under which loan purchases would be permitted.

We also believe the loan purchases did not meet the intent of the Act because the funds bailed out a failing company. The company had ceased operating about 3 weeks prior to the loan purchases, was in chapter 11 bankruptcy, and the prior lender was seeking to force the company into chapter 7 bankruptcy. There were also serious assertions made by the borrower's creditors that the company did not have a strong management team in place.[2] Therefore, we question whether using SSBCI funds to support a failing company met the intent of the program, which was to grow businesses and create jobs.

We noted that Michigan's application stated that "...generally, companies using the program would be otherwise strong, with typically modest historical cash flow coverage and typically strong indicators of future sales. They would also tend to have strong management teams in place, which the lender believes will perform well going forward in a normal collateral position." This wording of Michigan's application is so broad that it left a "loophole" by which the State could grant exceptions to the types of companies in which it would invest. While we believe there may be valid reasons for granting exceptions, exceptions should be documented and approved by Treasury to ensure that the intended use is for good cause and is consistent with the goals of the Act. Therefore, we believe that Treasury should modify Michigan's application to ensure the State is held accountable for making appropriate investments with its SSBCI funds. Treasury should also require states that make funding exceptions to their own stated policies to provide written justification for doing so.

Although the loan purchases constituted a misuse of funds because they did not meet the intent of the Act, we determined that they did

---

[2] The Official Committee of Unsecured Creditors of the company proffered allegations that two members of the company's board of directors "looted" the company, while the other three directors provided virtually no oversight.

not constitute intentional or reckless misuse. To conclude the misuse was reckless, the OIG would have to establish that Michigan should have known it was a misuse and that its actions constituted a highly unreasonable departure from the standards of ordinary care. Because Treasury guidelines did not address these types of transactions and the State's approved application was written in a way that could be broadly interpreted, we did not find that the misuse was reckless.

Michigan Spent $3,000 on a Loan Used for a Prohibited Business Purpose

Michigan paid $3,000 in SSBCI funds to a lender's reserve fund for a loan to be used for one business owner to buy out a partner. The Act requires that SSBCI loan proceeds be used for a "business purpose." A business purpose includes, but is not limited to, start-up costs, working capital, business procurement, franchise fees, equipment, and inventory, as well as the purchase, construction, renovation, or tenant improvements of an eligible place of business that is not for passive real estate investment purposes. Treasury guidelines state that loan proceeds will not be used to purchase any portion of an owner's interest in a business.

Treasury clearly prohibits such loans, but the enrollment form that State officials reviewed and signed did not disclose the loan's purpose. MEDC officials also informed us that its staff does not review loans enrolled in the CAP program to ensure the loans meet SSBCI criteria. Further, Treasury does not require the State to validate borrower/lender assurances regarding the uses of funds. Therefore, we cannot consider the misuse of the $3,000 to meet Treasury's definition of reckless or intentional.

However, we believe that allowing states to rely solely on lender and borrower assurances, without verifying the truth of the assurances, removes any accountability that states could have for preventing the misuse of SSBCI funds, which is not Treasury's intent. Also, while Treasury's national compliance standards[3] highlight additional actions

---

[3] *SSBCI National Standards for Compliance and Oversight,* effective as of May 15, 2012.

states can take to ensure that funds are used appropriately, such actions are not required. The absence of requirements prevents the OIG from classifying misuses of funds as reckless or intentional, and thus prevents Treasury from recouping misused funds. Therefore, at a minimum, we believe that Treasury should require states to use CAP program enrollment forms that disclose the purpose of loans enrolled. Doing so will ensure that states are aware of the intended uses of funds at the time of loan enrollment and provide the OIG with the proof needed to determine whether a misuse was intentional or reckless so that states can be held accountable.

Michigan Paid $21,000 for a CAP Loan Prior to the State's Admission to the SSBCI Program

We identified another loan that involved the misuse of $21,000 in SSBCI funds. Michigan paid $21,000 in SSBCI funds to the lender's reserve fund even though the loan was closed and funded on May 20, 2011 – almost 2 months prior to July 6, 2011, the date Michigan signed its Allocation Agreement. Therefore, the loan was not eligible for SSBCI funding.

The State's use of $21,000 to fund a loan that occurred prior to its acceptance into the SSBCI program met Treasury's definition of "reckless" misuse of funds, as the State was aware of its program admission date. The State had signed an Allocation Agreement with Treasury and received notification that it would receive its first allocation almost 2 months after the loan was funded. Additionally, the loan enrollment form was signed by three individuals, all of whom approved a transaction ineligible on its face. We can come to no conclusion other than that the review was carried on in a manner consciously indifferent to the quality of the review process or the likelihood that ineligible applications would be approved. Maintaining a review process lacking effective standards and/or quality control - evidenced by the individual approvals of not one, but three, reviewers and resulting in the misuse of SSBCI funds - exhibits gross indifference to the likelihood that ineligible transactions will be approved. This, in our view, constitutes a highly unreasonable departure from the standards of ordinary care.

Further, the loan in question already had been enrolled for 3½ months in the State's CAP program prior to being enrolled in the SSBCI program in September 2011. State officials also collected new borrower and lender assurances in September 2011, which provided another opportunity for the State to check the date the loan was funded.

Therefore, we find that Michigan's loan enrollment constituted a use of funds that the State or its administering entity knew or should have known was unauthorized or prohibited, and that its actions constituted a highly unreasonable departure from the standards of ordinary care. Because the Act requires recoupment of funds identified by the OIG as recklessly misused, Treasury will need to recover the $21,000 in misused funds associated with this loan.

A Portion of Administrative Costs Were Not Allowable or Allocable

Additionally, $8,506 in personnel costs incurred for administering SSBCI funds should be disallowed because such costs were incurred prior to Michigan's acceptance into the SSBCI program. We found that $8,506 out of $130,316 in administrative costs charged against SSBCI funds as of December 31, 2011, were not allowable or allocable to the program because the expenses were incurred prior to June 21, 2011, the date Michigan entered the program and was notified of its SSBCI allocation.

States may incur administrative costs beginning on the date of the Allocation Agreement, which constitutes the beginning of the award period and the date that Treasury establishes its obligation to the state. However, Michigan initially charged SSBCI for its May and June 2011 personnel costs for three staff members working on the SSBCI program. While the State subsequently reversed the costs for two of the staff members, it overlooked the cost for a third. According to OMB Circular A-87, pre-award costs are allowable only when they would have been allowable if incurred after the date of the award and only with written approval of the awarding agency. Michigan did not request, and did not receive, written approval from Treasury for the pre-award of these administrative costs. Therefore,

Treasury should disallow the $8,506 in pre-award administrative expenses.

Recommendations

We recommend that the Deputy Assistant Secretary for Small Business, Housing, and Community Development:

1. Issue guidance addressing the conditions under which loan purchase transactions would be permitted.

   Management Response

   Treasury agreed with this recommendation and will issue guidance addressing the conditions under which loan purchase transactions would be permitted. However, Treasury noted that it authorized Michigan's use of funds for purchasing loan participations and stated that the transactions identified as misuse constituted new extensions of credit that refinanced the debt of an unaffiliated lender.

   OIG Comment

   We consider Treasury's action to be responsive to our recommendation. However, we disagree with Treasury's assessment that the questioned transactions constituted refinancing of existing debt by an unaffiliated lender, which is permitted. Industry practice has shown that a refinancing involves new loan documents, a credit analysis, appraisal of collateral, and a review of financial statements of the business. None of these were present for the transactions questioned. The loan purchases legally were an "Assignment and Assumption" of debt, and were simply a transfer of debt obligations from one financial institution to another, not unlike a lender selling a home mortgage to another financial institution with no involvement by the borrower. Therefore, we question whether the loan purchase transactions were consistent with the intent of the Act to increase capital to small businesses to allow them to expand, grow, and create jobs.

   While Treasury has not defined refinancing of existing debt for the purposes of this program, SSBCI Policy Guidelines require that new monies must be advanced to the borrower when the same or affiliated lenders refinance prior debt. This change in SSBCI guidelines was made in response to our September 2012 report on *Montana's Use of Funds Received from the State Small Business Credit Initiative.* This report pointed out that allowing SSBCI funds to be used on refinancing with no limits on the amount being refinanced could result in little new capital being extended to small businesses and may allow prior debt to be brought under the protection of the SSBCI program. Although Treasury guidelines are silent as to whether the requirement to advance new monies should be imposed on loans refinanced by different lenders, it would be logical and prudent to apply the same criteria to such transactions for the same reasons Treasury changed its policy on refinancing prior debt from the same lender.

2. Require Michigan to modify its SSBCI application to acknowledge that when it invests in companies that do not meet the representations made in its application, it must document its rationale for doing so and seek approval from Treasury to ensure the transaction meets the intent of the Act.

   Management Response

   Treasury agreed with this recommendation and will require Michigan to acknowledge that it will document and seek approval for any use of funds that differs from its original SSBCI application.

   OIG Comment

   We consider Treasury's action to be responsive to our recommendation.

3. Require states that grant funds as an exception to their own stated policies to provide written justification for doing so.

   Management Response

   Treasury agreed with this recommendation and will require states that use SSBCI funds in ways that differ from their applications to provide written justification for doing so.

OIG Comment

We consider Treasury's action to be responsive to our recommendation.

4. Require states to use enrollment forms for CAP programs that disclose the purpose of loans enrolled.

   Management Response

   Treasury agreed with this recommendation and will require states to use enrollment forms for CAP programs that disclose the purpose of loans.

   OIG Comment

   We consider Treasury's action to be responsive to our recommendation.

5. Recoup from the State of Michigan $21,000 of recklessly misused funds for the loan that occurred prior to Michigan's participation in the SSBCI program.

   Management Response

   Treasury agreed with this recommendation and will recoup from Michigan $21,000 for enrolling a loan that the financial institution closed prior to Michigan's participation in the program. Treasury also noted that it does not believe all instances of inadvertent errors in enrolling a loan necessarily meet the published definition of reckless misuse.

   OIG Comment

   We consider Treasury's action to be responsive to our recommendation. We also wish to emphasize that Michigan's enrollment of a loan made prior to its participation in SSBCI was not an "inadvertent" error. The loan had been enrolled for 3½ months in the State's CAP program and had to be removed from the CAP program and re-enrolled in the SSBCI program, with new borrower and lender assurances. Also the re-enrollment was evidenced by three State reviewers, each of which signed the

SSBCI loan enrollment form showing the significant time gap between the date the loan was made and when it was enrolled in the SSBCI program.

6. Disallow the $8,506 in administrative expenses incurred prior to June 21, 2011.

Management Response

Treasury agreed with this recommendation and will disallow the $8,506 in impermissible administrative expenses.

OIG Comment

We consider Treasury's action to be responsive to our recommendation.

* * * * * *

We appreciate the courtesies and cooperation provided to our staff during the evaluation. If you wish to discuss the report, you may contact me at (202) 622-1090 or Lisa DeAngelis, Audit Director, at (202) 927-5621.

/s/
Debra Ritt
Special Deputy Inspector General for
Office of Small Business Lending Fund Program Oversight

Appendix 1: Objective, Scope, and Methodology

The objective of our audit was to test participant compliance with program requirements and prohibitions to identify reckless or intentional misuse of funds. As of March 31, 2012, Michigan had obligated or spent $38,566,045 in State Small Business Credit Initiative (SSBCI) funds through its participating programs, including $340,901 for insurance premiums through the Michigan Capital Access Program (CAP), 38,026,333 for collateral support and loan participations through the Michigan Business Growth Fund, and $198,811 for costs associated with administering the State programs. An additional program, the Small Business Mezzanine Fund, with authorized funds totaling $6 million had not spent or obligated any SSBCI funds.

The scope of our audit included small business loans enrolled in the Michigan CAP and loans made by the Michigan Business Growth Fund, which were supported by SSBCI funds (either in the form of collateral support or direct loan participations) during the period, June 21, 2011 (the date Michigan was approved for the program) to December 31, 2011. During this period, the Michigan CAP and the Michigan Business Growth Fund had enrolled or supported 113 loans with a total loan value of $71,936,256. The total Federal contribution to the loan reserve funds associated with the CAP loans amounted to $196,989. The total SSBCI funds used in support of the Michigan Business Growth Fund's other credit support programs amounted to $29,725,594.

We interviewed Michigan Economic Development Corporation (MEDC) staff with responsibility for administering the Michigan CAP and the Michigan Business Growth Fund on behalf of the MSF to understand and assess:

- Whether the State used its allocated funding under the program in accordance with its approved application;

- Procedures in place to process small business loans and ensure compliance with the requirements of the Act and associated Treasury guidelines; and

- Accounting and reporting processes, including methodologies for calculating and reporting administrative expenses.

In addition, we also reviewed associated policies, procedures, and other written guidance provided by The Michigan CAP and the Michigan Business Growth Fund related to the use of SSBCI funds.

We selected a sample of loans enrolled in the Michigan CAP and the Michigan Business Growth Fund as of December 31, 2011, and performed testing to ensure such loans complied with the requirements and prohibitions of the Act and associated Treasury guidelines. We used a statistical sampling methodology for 59 of the loans and judgmentally selected one more loan based on the complexities noted in a similar loan to the borrower.

We selected 23 loans enrolled in the Michigan Business Growth Fund for our review. These 23 loans were originated by 12 lending institutions throughout Michigan. During May 2012, we conducted an on-site review of loan files at the MEDC and compared the documentation in the loan files to specific requirements and prohibitions of the Act and associated Treasury guidelines. MEDC staff provided loan files supporting our review of collateral support or loan participation activity in the OCSP programs.

We selected 36 loans enrolled in the Michigan CAP for review. Eight lending institutions throughout Michigan originated the 36 loans, for which the Michigan Strategic Fund paid the associated insurance premiums, and MEDC provided administration support. During May 2012, we conducted an on-site review of the CAP loan files at the MEDC and compared the documentation in the loan files to specific requirements and prohibitions of the Act and associated Treasury guidelines. Lender institutions and MEDC staff provided the CAP loan files directly or by electronic means.

We conducted our audit between April 2012 and November 2012 in accordance with Government Auditing Standards. Those standards require that we plan and perform the audit to obtain sufficient, appropriate evidence to provide a reasonable basis for our findings and conclusions based on our audit objectives. We believe that the evidence obtained to address our audit objectives provides a reasonable basis for our findings and conclusions.

Appendix 2: Management Response

DEPARTMENT OF THE TREASURY
WASHINGTON, D.C. 20220

December 6, 2012

Debra Ritt
Special Deputy Inspector General for
 Office of Small Business Lending Fund Program Oversight
U.S. Department of the Treasury
1500 Pennsylvania Avenue, NW
Washington, DC 20220

Dear Ms. Ritt:

Thank you for the opportunity to review the Office of the Inspector General's (OIG) draft report entitled *Michigan's Use of Funds Received from the State Small Business Credit Initiative* (the Report). This letter provides the official response of the Department of the Treasury (Treasury).

We appreciate the Report's finding that Michigan used the majority of State Small Business Credit Initiative (SSBCI) funds properly, and that a large majority of sampled loans complied with SSBCI program requirements. However, the Report also identifies some instances of non-compliance. In response, with your consent, Treasury transmitted a revised copy of the Report to Michigan program officials on November 19, 2012. Treasury directed Michigan to submit a written reply describing the remedial measures Michigan has taken or plans to take to address the deficiencies noted in the Report, including those related to use of funds and administrative costs.

Michigan's reply, enclosed, states that "[Michigan's] actions to implement and operate the programs were, and continue to be, performed professionally and with the utmost of good faith," and that Michigan "respectfully disagree[s] with the OIG conclusions that the MPI loan participation of $2.5 million represents a misuse, and that any reckless misuse occurred."

Treasury accepts each of the Report's recommendations. Regarding recommendations 1, 2 and 3, Treasury will issue guidance addressing the conditions under which loan purchase transactions would be permitted. Treasury will require Michigan to acknowledge that it will document and seek approval for any use of funds that differs from its original SSBCI application. More generally, Treasury will require states that use SSBCI funds in a way that differs from its application to provide written justification for doing so.

Treasury notes that "misuse" of funds is defined in published guidance to mean "any use . . . that is not an authorized use or is a prohibited use under the [Small Business Jobs] Act." Treasury authorized the program described in Michigan's application which included the purchase of participations in credit facilities. In addition, Michigan's purchase of a loan participation in a credit facility was not a prohibited use of funds under the Act. The borrower benefitted from this transaction through reduced borrowing costs and its ability to attract subsequent financing, ultimately re-hiring workers who were previously laid off. The essential nature of the transaction was a new extension of credit that refinanced the debt of an unaffiliated lender.

1

When Michigan used SSBCI funds to purchase a participation in the new lender's loan, its actions were consistent with its state program as approved by Treasury.

Regarding recommendations 4 and 5, Treasury will require states to use enrollment forms for CAP programs that disclose the purpose of loans enrolled and will recoup from Michigan $21,000 for enrolling a loan that the financial institution closed prior to Michigan's participation in the program. Treasury notes that it does not believe all instances of inadvertent errors in enrolling a loan necessarily meet the published definition of a "reckless" misuse of funds.

Finally, in accord with recommendation 6, Treasury will disallow $8,506 in administrative expenses. Michigan's reply states that those costs were charged in error, and agrees that the expenses are impermissible.

Thank you once again for the opportunity to review the Report. Treasury appreciates our work together throughout the course of the SSBCI program.

Sincerely,

Don Graves, Jr.
Deputy Assistant Secretary for Small Business, Community Development, and Affordable Housing Policy

Enclosure

MICHIGAN STRATEGIC FUND

300 N Washington Sq
Lansing, MI 48913

MSF BOARD

Michael A. Finney
*Chairperson***
*President and Chief
Executive Officer,
(MSF Board President
and Chairman)
Michigan Economic
Development Corporation*

Steven Hilfinger,
Director
*Michigan Department of
Licensing & Regulatory
Affairs*

Andy Dillon */**
*State Treasurer
Michigan Department
of Treasury*

Paul Hodges, III*
Citizen

Michael J. Jackson, Sr.**
*Executive Secretary,
Michigan Regional
Council of Carpenters*

Sabrina E. Keeley
*Chief Operational Officer,
Business Leaders for
Michigan*

Bill J. Martin **
*Chief Executive Officer,
Michigan Association
of REALTORS*

William Morris***
*President/Chief Investment
Officer,
Prairie & Tireman, LLC*

James C. Petcoff */**
President, JPFS, LLC

Richard Rassel***
*Director of Global Client
Relations, Butzel Long*

Shaun W. Wilson
*Vice President/Director of
Client and Community
Relations, PNC Financial
Services Group*

*MSF Investment
Subcommittee member

**MSF Incentive
Subcommittee member

***MSF Entrepreneurial
Subcommittee member

November 27, 2012

Mr. Don J. Graves, Jr.
Deputy Assistant Secretary for Small Business,
Community Development and Housing Policy
Department of the Treasury
Washington, D.C. 20220

VIA ELECTRONIC MAIL

Dear Mr. Graves:

Thank you for providing the Michigan Strategic Fund ("MSF") the opportunity to respond to your most recent letter dated November 19, 2012, surrounding the allegations of United States Department of Treasury ("US Treasury") Office of the Inspector General ("OIG") in its draft report, received on November 19, 2012 and dated November xx, 2012, entitled, *"Michigan's Use of Funds Received from the State Small Business Credit Initiative"* ("SSBCI") ("Report").

Over 25 years ago, the MSF began successfully operating its state funded capital access program. In addition, prior to the passage of the SSBCI Act in 2010 the MSF created and began successfully operating its own state funded collateral support and loan participation programs. The state funding for these Michigan programs was quickly depleted due to the enormous demand. Due to the success of Michigan's programs, the MSF was instrumental in assisting US Treasury and Congress to form the parameters of the capital access program ("CAP"), and other credit support program ("OCSP") of the SSBCI Act. Michigan's programs were literally the model for much of SSBCI. Because of these efforts, all states have been given the opportunity to use SSBCI to benefit their businesses and employees, and continue to help our nation recover from the devastating recession.

The MSF is very pleased with the outstanding success of its own state funded capital access, loan participation and collateral support programs, as well as the federally funded CAP and OCSP counterparts, and the economic benefit realized for our state. To date, the SSBCI programs have involved 250+ credit facilities, supported by approximately $42.6 million of SSBCI funds **without a single credit facility loss**. Without the SSBCI programs, the businesses assisted would most likely not have been able to weather the economic strife Michigan has experienced. Overall, the SSBCI support has resulted in approximately $207 million of private leverage, returned approximately $7 million in principal, fees, and interest to Michigan's SSBCI programs, and is projected to create and/or retain approximately 3,900 employees.

Since the inception of the SSBCI programs, the MSF has taken the need for internal controls over the programs very seriously. Prior to the creation and operation of the SSBCI programs, both process development and the transaction documents were the subjects of careful, conscientious, and oftentimes forward thinking. Staff with various expertise has gone to great lengths to educate themselves to review, understand, and dissect the initial guidelines and Frequently Asked Questions ("FAQs") offered by US Treasury. These efforts have continued with the revisions that have been published by US Treasury over time as the programs have grown nationwide, more questions and issues have arisen, and the practical impact of the programs has become apparent. US Treasury has been helpful in many instances to assist the MSF remain updated, on track, and within the intent and purpose of the programs. The MSF strongly believes that all actions to implement and operate the programs were, and continue to be, performed professionally and with the utmost of good faith.

Your letter requests that Michigan provide a narrative response describing remedial measures that Michigan has taken or plans to take to address the "deficiencies" noted by the OIG in the Report. OIG claims that $2.524 million of SSBCI funds was "misused". Of that $2.524 million, OIG claims the use of approximately $21,000 amounted to "reckless misuse."

While we appreciate the opportunity to respond specifically to the allegations of OIG in the Report and your requests, we respectfully disagree with the OIG conclusions that the MPI loan participation of $2.5 million represents a misuse, and that any reckless misuse occurred. The facts are that of the $2.524 million in claims by the OIG, only approximately $24,000 was misused and none of those results were reckless.

Prior to providing this response, we traveled to Washington, D.C. to meet with OIG staff. We provided paperwork and offered detailed discussion in an effort to ensure OIG staff understood relevant facts of the underlying transactions in question and the guidelines that were available to Michigan under the emerging SSBCI programs. We requested reconsideration of the written determinations in OIG's original draft report dated August 24, 2012. We are pleased that OIG has made substantial changes to its findings evidenced by this latest Report. Unfortunately the latest Report still contains incorrect facts and interpretations of program guidelines and levels of misuse. Thus, the MSF will do its best in this letter to respond to the Report by examining OIG's specific claims, where they can be discerned, and to those OIG conclusions which can only be described as general or impressionistic.

The findings in the Report indicate OIG has not accurately interpreted the guidelines and levels of misuse of the SSBCI programs and lacks full understanding of the facts of the underlying loans it believes are at issue. Further, the Report claims misuse based on guidelines that are not cited and do not exist, and delves into areas of review which are outside of the purview of the OIG, such as relative risk of an individual credit decision. OIG's determination of alleged reckless misuse is supported by incorrect factual findings and could cause serious and unfounded damage to the reputation of the MSF.

The MSF understands that the following are the relevant standards of review of use of SSBCI funds developed by Treasury in conjunction with the OIG:

(i) Misuse: (i) any use of allocated funds under the control of the participating state or its administering entities identified in Annex 1 of the Allocation Agreement that is not an authorized use or is a prohibited use under the SSBCI, the Allocation Agreement, or the program guidelines; or (ii) any act of omission that enables other parties, including administering entities identified in Annex 1 of the Allocation Agreement, to misuse allocated funds; and

(ii) Reckless misuse: use of allocated funds that the participating state or its administering entity should have known was unauthorized or prohibited. A reckless misuse of funds is a highly unreasonable departure or willful disregard from the standards of ordinary care, and may be a single instance or a series of instances.

To effectively respond to the conclusions of the OIG, the SSBCI Act, SSBCI guidelines, and SSBCI FAQs, as applicable, must be analyzed to determine the "rules", then facts must exist to support that the MSF engaged in misuse, reckless misuse or intentional misuse, as alleged by the OIG. The OIG fails to set forth the correct "rules", fails to support its claims of misuse in some instances, and fails to support its claim of reckless, as no such facts exist.

OIG Finding #1 (Report, page 7): "Michigan Business Growth Fund Financed $2.5 Million Lender Purchases that Did Not Extend Credit to Borrowers"

OIG's first finding is in regards to Michigan's participation under the state's SSBCI Michigan Business Growth Fund–Michigan Loan Participation Program with mBank, a small Michigan bank based in Manistique, Michigan, which provided loans to Manistique Papers, Inc. ("MPI") in August 2011. MPI operated the county's largest private-sector employer, a paper mill. MPI had several notes for working capital and long term debt with the Royal Bank of Scotland ("RBS") totaling over $11.1 million. RBS had a first priority lien on virtually all of the effective assets of MPI. MPI had been working with RBS seeking additional working capital and considerations to avoid acceleration of the underlying RBS indebtedness. Having no success with RBS, and facing liquidation by RBS, MPI filed for Chapter 11 bankruptcy protection. As a consequence, all the outstanding principal and interest owed to RBS was effectively accelerated. RBS was in the process of requesting chapter 7 liquidation of MPI's assets through proper bankruptcy court channels to satisfy the indebtedness, when MPI requested mBank and the MSF's involvement. With the support of the SSBCI funds, mBank refinanced four (4) MPI debts held by RBS, which totaled approximately $7.67 million in new exposure for mBank. The MSF participated in two (2) of those restructurings. The MSF provided $2 million (or 48.27%) of the support of a refinanced $4,142,889 note and $500,000 (or 37.5%) of the support of a refinanced $1,333,348 note.

OIG's finding seems to be based on two (2) distinct sub-claims set forth in the Report. **First, it appears that OIG concluded that the transaction "did not provide new credit or a cash infusion to the borrower, but rather transferred an existing loan from one lender to another."** Report, page 7. **Second, it appears the OIG believes the MPI transactions were too risky.** *"We believe the loan*

3

purchases did not meet the intent of the Act because the funds bailed out a failing company." Report, page 8. Thus, it appears OIG has concluded that the mBank loans represented a higher credit risk than MSF's SSBCI Application to US Treasury dated June 20, 2011 ("Application") implied it would be taking.

Based on the above claims, OIG concludes that the MSF's use of $2.5 million in SSBCI funds to support mBank's extensions of credit to MPI is a "misuse". Discussed below are the facts in relation to OIG's claim.

New Extension of Credit. OIG does not cite what portion of the SSBCI Act, guidelines, or FAQs applies. In fact, OIG acknowledges that the transaction was allowable according to Treasury guidelines and the MSF application. The OIG claim seems to be based on a disagreement with Treasury over the "intent" of the program. Lacking actual language in the Act or guidelines to cite, the Report states..."While the transactions temporarily kept the borrower from defaulting on its two loans, we question whether loan purchases are consistent with the intent of the Act to increase capital to allow small businesses to expand, grow and create jobs." However, Treasury's existing guidelines and responses to FAQs r clearly permitted this type of transaction. Section XII of the then existing Treasury guidelines (April 27, 2011) provides that funds made available to states under SSBCI will be permitted to support only new extensions of credit, that is, not to support refinancing of existing credit by the **same or affiliated lender**. The rule is explained by the guidance provided in the then existing FAQs (Post Award/Compliance Questions, response to FAQ #2, May 2011, page 8) which "does not prohibit a financial institution lender from enrolling or refinancing previously made loans from another, non-affiliated financial institution into an approved program".

As noted above, with the support of the SSBCI funds, mBank refinanced four (4) MPI debts held by RBS, which totaled approximately $7.67 million in new exposure for mBank. RBS was not, or is not, affiliated in any way with mBank. The MSF participated in two (2) of those restructurings. The OIG seemingly is "hung-up" on the mechanics of the credit extended to MPI by mBank, and ignores the new credit terms extended by mBank. The credit terms extended by mBank to restructure the RBS notes were unique from the RBS notes, and beneficial to the borrower (MPI), in every pertinent way. The new credit was for a unique extended term, lower interest rate, and lower principal amount. mBank, the new lender, and MPI, the borrower, agreed that the maturity date would be extended for a 4 month period, and the interest rate would be WSJP (3.25%) + 1% with a floor of 4.25%, compared to the RBS notes which had been declared in default and due and carried an interest rate at 8.75%. In addition, the parties understood that the discount paid by mBank for the purchase of the RBS notes would be passed through to MPI when a new investor to purchase the assets was found. The $2.2 million discount to the original loans was passed on to MPI when the sale of the assets finally did occur several months later.

The MSF would also like to point out that the transaction in question meets OIG's interpretation that the Act intended to "increase capital to the borrower to allow small businesses to expand, grow and create jobs." Michigan's $2.5 million participation allowed MPI to avoid chapter 7 liquidation, continue to benefit from $11.1 million in term debt, cut MPI's interest rates by half, cut its owed principal by $2.2

4

million, facilitated access to $5 million in working capital (a month later), helped restart the factory, "expanded" and promoted product diversification, and helped to "create [nearly 100] jobs." (MPI went from a moth-ball workforce of just over 30 to 125 within a month.)

OIG goes on to use this Report to argue its interpretation of the "intent" of the Act. "If such transactions are allowed, SSBCI funds could be used to largely finance repeated loan purchases that do not increase the amount of capital extended to small businesses. While Treasury considers an increase in credit on a lender's books to constitute "new credit," regardless of whether the small business is advanced new monies, viewing this issue solely from the lender perspective could lead to sanctioning transactions that result in no net increases in lending or capital to small businesses." "Thus, the transaction was not unlike a lender selling a home mortgage to another financial institution with no involvement by the borrower." OIG's fact and analogy are incorrect and its concern is unfounded.

MPI led this refinancing effort. It was MPI that approached the MSF and mBank, requesting help. Businesses only seek a new lender to refinance existing debt, if it is a benefit to the business. Most examples of this type of transaction are not as dramatically positive as the MPI transaction. In this banking crisis, banks commonly want out of a loan because they need to increase cash on their balance sheet, or have industry or geographic concentration. These banks occasionally take relatively healthy companies into bankruptcy to liquidate assets, but more commonly call the loan for some minor covenant breach. This is a huge issue around the country, but especially in Michigan. Companies facing this type of loss of credit would go out of business if they could not refinance their debt before being thrown out by their old lender. The ability of these businesses to take advantage of the SSBCI program absolutely gives these businesses the ability to expand, grow and create jobs.

Application to US Treasury by MSF. As for OIG's claim that the MPI support was a deviation from the "intent of the Act" and how Michigan portrayed its program to Treasury, and thus, its inference that the MPI support was too risky, the MSF relies on its Application which provides, in part:

> "Generally, companies using this program are otherwise strong, with typically modest historical cash flow coverage and typically strong indicators of future sales. They also tend to have strong management teams in place which the lender believes will perform well going forward and a normal collateral position. Those aspects make the loan transaction attractive to the bank but for a weakness in cash flow coverage related to a diversification investment or some performance problem during the broader economic downturn or issues potentially related to customer or product concentration risk which the bank finds unacceptable." Application, Attachment to Section 4A.

OIG states that these transactions by the MSF violated the "intent of the Act." *"We also believe the loan purchases did not meet the intent of the Act because the funds bailed out a failing company." "Therefore, we question whether using SSBCI funds to support a failing company met the intent of the program, which was to grow businesses and create jobs."* Report, page 8 We strongly disagree with the OIG's assessment of MPI as a "failing" company. We encourage OIG staff to visit MPI and its current

5

130+ well paid employees. Clearly, the support for the MPI loans represented exactly what the Act intended and the MSF portrayed to US Treasury as cited above.

The MSF, in its extensive due diligence process, saw that the paper production business is traditionally cyclical. The bankruptcy was caused by a short turn in the market of feed stock, the market for high gloss paper, and the impatience of MPI's then current lender, RBS. While immediate cash flows were an issue for MPI, the mill had a history of cash flow. The company had been in existence for over 90 years and was attempting to adapt to market conditions to diversify products and customers to enhance future sales when its then current lender was unwilling to continue its relationship with the company. RBS was using some short term covenant breaches to precipitate its exit from the loan.

Both mBank and MSF performed extensive due diligence on the company's indicators of future sales, collateral values and management team. The skilled management team in place at the MSF investment, continue to be the same management team responsible for the success of the business today. The Board members in question in the OIG report cited in footnote 1 on page 8 had been removed, and the MSF and mBank vetted the managers on their performance and deemed them to be very skilled, effective and having the ability to manage the company's turn-around. The MSF provided the OIG with the resumes of the managers, and the results speak for themselves. The assessment of the managers by mBank, the MSF and Bankruptcy Court was correct.

Unfortunately, OIG never cites a rule or guideline which was violated and delves into areas of review which are outside of the purview of the OIG. OIG's claim that questions the decision to support a company taking full advantage of a Chapter 11 protection proceedings second guesses mBank's and the MSF's credit decision. OIG does not seem to realize that knowing a company is in chapter 11 may be informative about its relative health, but it is not determinative and one must do further due diligence in order to determine if it is "failing" from a credit risk perspective.

OIG's assertion that MPI was a "failing" business and that MSF's support of the MPI refinancing was irresponsible is clearly refuted when one considers: (i) credit decisions are outside the purview of the OIG, (ii) OIG's assessment is exactly opposite of the expert, self-interested decision makers (mBank, MSF, the bankruptcy court which oversaw and approved all MPI dealings with mBank, and the numerous secured and unsecured claimants of MPI in the bankruptcy proceedings), and (iii) the actual results of the transaction and performance of the loan and company, which were known at the time of the OIG review. (The company had restarted, tripled the number of employees, was beating their sales and profit numbers, exited from bankruptcy, and paid back the MSF loans in question in full plus fees.) The various interested parties performed extensive due diligence on the viability of the company's plan and its collateral value. The exact plan to diversify and hopefully bring in a new investor for the company worked, and the successful operations of the paper mill have continued.

The Report also makes a circular argument, appearing to claim that the credit decision was both too risky and at the same time, implying that RBS, mBank and MSF were seemingly improperly guaranteed to be paid back at great benefit to the lenders, by a pre-negotiated sale.

> *"The loan purchases also benefitted the prior lender by removing bad loans from its books. The new lender benefitted too by recouping, with interest, the funds it had loaned when the borrower's business was sold months after the loan purchases. Finally, the State recouped the SSBCI funds used to purchase the loans." Report page 7*

The Report made note that the transaction removed a bad loan off of RBS's books and the negotiated sale of the company resulted in mBank and MSF being paid back. Again, OIG does not cite any guideline prohibiting prior lender and current lender from being repaid and misrepresents the facts. RBS being able to remove the loan off of its books is not impermissible. This was also what was going to happen had the chapter 7 liquidation occurred, except the company and jobs would be gone. It should be noted that RBS had to take a $2.2 million dollar write-down, which was passed through to MPI, in order to get the benefit of "removing the loans from its books." A lender and MSF being paid back, with interest and fees, is not only permissible, it is the goal in almost every SSBCI transaction. OIG's notion that a sale was in anyway pre-negotiated is patently false. In fact, the sale of the assets to the new investor took place eight months after the closing of the loans. Not "months" as stated in the Report and was only completed after:

- Hiring an investor bank to market and sell the company
- Creating a deal package
- Marketing the company
- Vetting potential bidders, including a court-approved stalking horse bidder
- Conducting a court-approved auction
- Negotiating and executing a court-approved purchase agreement with many contingencies that had to be met
- Closing the transaction

All of the above steps resulted in the payoff of all of the mBank credit facilities to MPI, including the two (2) facilities criticized by OIG.

It should be noted, the Report was factually incorrect when it stated "…(although the company remains in chapter 11 bankruptcy)…". In fact, in the first year after the MSF's support, MPI has hired approximately 100 employees, come out of bankruptcy, MSF has been paid back $2.5 million of its SSBCI funds plus $75,000 in fees, MPI has carried an annual payroll of $8.1 million plus annual benefits of $4.1 million, and made local purchases of goods and services of approximately $30 million. All of these events had occurred prior to the OIG's review of the loans.

In summary, there was no misuse. Michigan is glad to be "held accountable for making appropriate investment [like MPI] with [our] SSBCI funds." The MPI loans in question were permitted refinancing by the Act and guidelines. The loans were consistent with the MSF's application. MPI was the exact

type of company and opportunity the Act intended. Many of Michigan's congressional delegation, including the Act's sponsoring members, have cited MPI as an example of this program's great successes.

OIG Finding #2 (Report, page 9): "Michigan Spent $3,000 on a Loan Used for a Prohibited Business Purpose"

This OIG finding stems from one loan. OIG claims the loan was supported with SSBCI funds totaling $3,000 for loan proceeds used to finance a prohibited partner buy-out.

This is correct. However, prior to the support being provided by the MSF, the borrower signed written assurances to the MSF that the loan would not be used for that prohibited purpose. Nothing in the Act, guidelines, May 2011 FAQs or April 2012 FAQs require independent verification by the MSF of borrower assurances as to the use of proceeds. The SSBCI National Standards for Compliance and Oversight, released after this loan was made, state "while Treasury does not require Participating States (or administering entities, lenders, or investors, if so designated) to independently verify the representations made by the authorized representative of the small business borrower or investee with respect to the use of proceeds, Treasury does expect Participating States, as part of their compliance monitoring procedures, to establish a process to determine whether these required certifications have been adequately documented". The MSF process, which was followed in this case and has been in place since the inception of the SSBCI programs, exactly follows the process recommended by US Treasury but goes further and requires borrower assurances are made directly to the MSF.

OIG recommends that Treasury require states to use a CAP enrollment form which requires the bank/borrower to state the purpose of the loan. We believe this is a good suggestion and have already implemented the required disclosure on our CAP enrollment form.

OIG Finding #3 (Report, page 10): "Michigan Paid $21,000 for a CAP Loan Prior to State's Admission to the SSBCI Program"

OIG found that MSF had enrolled a loan in the SSBCI CAP which had been closed before the date on which MSF signed our SSBCI allocation agreement. OIG concluded that this represented a "reckless misuse" of funds. This misuse does not rise to the level of a reckless misuse, but was an administrative error in an otherwise robust process. OIG cites incorrect facts in its justification for holding this misuse to rise to the high standard of reckless.

Contrary to the Report, the loan in question had not "been enrolled for 3 1/2 months in the State's CAP program prior to being enrolled in the SSBCI program in September 2011..." The program administrators inadvertently, overlooked the date of the bank's closing. MSF has a robust process in place to prevent enrolling loans in SSBCI which were closed prior to MSF signing of their Allocation Agreement. OIG correctly pointed out that the MSF process includes three checks for compliance. Any process of this type must have a human element. Any process with a human element cannot have 100% accuracy.

MSF was processing two to six CAP loans per week during this time, with almost 100% accuracy. Unfortunately human error occurred in the processing of the loan in question resulting in the misuse. It is inappropriate to hold MSF's actions as "reckless", from a single, inadvertent human error. The MSF plans to dis-enroll this loan from the SSBCI program and enroll it in the State's CAP program.

OIG Finding #4 (Report, page 11): "A Portion of Administrative Costs Were Not Allowable or Allocable"

The OIG states that $8,506 in personnel costs incurred for administering SSBCI funds should be disallowed because such costs were incurred prior to Michigan's acceptance into the SSBCI program. There was no intent to improperly allocate personnel costs. A new staff member was hired in May 2011 specifically to devote 100% of his time to implementing the new SSBCI program. His time from May to mid-June 2011 was improperly charged as an administrative expense. This was an administrative error to charge these personnel costs to the program and we agree that these costs should be disallowed.

Remedial Measures

US Treasury has asked the MSF to comment on specific remedial measures to address the alleged deficiencies noted in the Report.

1. **Efforts to address use of proceeds for partner buy-out**

The MSF already requires the borrower to certify directly to the MSF that the underlying loan is not being used to purchase any portion of an owner's interest in the business. The MSF has revised the CAP enrollment forms to require a detailed explanation of the use of proceeds of the underlying loan. As to the $3,000 SSBCI support improperly used, we have notified the lender that the underlying loan was used for a prohibited purpose and it has been dis-enrolled from the SSBCI program and the funds have been removed from the lender's CAP reserve account.

2. **Efforts to ensure proper administrative charges**

The MSF has and will continue to document each staff member's time on a bi-weekly timesheet. Time worked on SSBCI programs is recorded by hours worked each pay cycle. The error made in prematurely charging a new staff member's time to the SSBCI programs before the Allocation Agreement was signed is a one-time occurrence. The MSF has corrected the $8,506 overcharge by netting out these costs from the MSF's SSBCI third quarter ending allowed administrative expenses.

3. **Ensure all funds are used in a manner consistent with our Application**

The MSF strongly believes that every transaction supported by SSBCI dollars was completely within the stated intent and purpose of the program as outlined in our Application. The MSF has always and will continue to review every transaction to ensure compliance. The MSF does not believe the Application needs modification. If Treasury believes that the MSF stepped outside the purview of its Application, the MSF respectfully requests further discussion with Treasury about potential modifications to the Application that Treasury believes are warranted.

In conclusion, the MSF does not agree with the OIG's assessment of the handling of the SSBCI program. The conclusion of reckless misuse is completely unfounded.

Sincerely,

Michael A. Finney

Michael A. Finney
Chairperson
Michigan Strategic Fund

Appendix 3: Major Contributors

Debra Ritt, Special Deputy Inspector General

Lisa DeAngelis, Audit Director

Clayton Boyce, Audit Director

John Rizek, Audit Manager

Andrew Morgan, Auditor-in-Charge

Safal Bhattarai, Auditor

Appendix 4: Distribution List

Department of the Treasury
Deputy Secretary
Office of Strategic Planning and Performance Management
Risk and Control Group

Office of Management and Budget
OIG Budget Examiner

United States Senate
Chairman and Ranking Member
Committee on Small Business and Entrepreneurship

Chairman and Ranking Member
Committee on Finance

Chairman and Ranking Member
Committee on Banking, Housing and Urban Affairs

United States House of Representatives
Chairman and Ranking Member
Committee on Small Business

Chairman and Ranking Member
Committee on Financial Services

Government Accountability Office
Comptroller General of the United States

www.ingramcontent.com/pod-product-compliance
Lightning Source LLC
Chambersburg PA
CBHW081807170526
45167CB00008B/3362